# For His Glory
## Jacqueline James

✝

**PUBLISHED by PARABLES**
*Earthly Stories with a Heavenly Meaning*

For His Glory
Copyright ©Jacqueline James
November, 2021

*Published By Parables*

All Rights Reserved. No part of this book may be reproduced or utilized in any form or by any means, electronic or mechanical, including photocopying, recording, or by any information storage and retrieval system, without permission in writing from the author.

Unless otherwise specified Scripture quotations are taken from the authorized version of the King James Bible.

Readers should be aware that Internet Web sites offered as citations and/or sources for further information may have been changed or disappeared between the time this was written and when it is read.

Printed in the United States of America

# For His Glory
## Jacqueline James

**PUBLISHED by PARABLES**
Earthly Stories with a Heavenly Meaning

## Table of Content.

### Glorify the Lord

| | |
|---|---|
| 1. God gets His Glory | 10 |
| 2. I am of God…God is of me | 11 |
| 3. God Rock | 13 |
| 4. Jesus is | 14 |
| 5. Infinite Blessing | 16 |
| 6. God is Blessing me | 17 |
| 7. 5-Star Faith | 18 |
| 8. God on my Mind | 19 |
| 9. Do it for me Lord | 20 |
| 10. God is the Author of my Faith | 21 |
| 11. Thankful | 22 |

### Revive me Lord

| | |
|---|---|
| 1. Empty me Lord now fill me up | 28 |
| 2. Your Love for me Lord | 29 |
| 3. Peace me to be Still | 30 |
| 4. Have a Clear Heart for God | 32 |
| 5. Empty am I | 34 |
| 6. Restore my Faith | 35 |
| 7. Lost Souls | 36 |
| 8. He's a Healer | 38 |
| 9. Please Lord Have Mercy | 39 |
| 10. A Reason to Pray | 40 |
| 11. My Faith is Strong | 41 |

## God is in Control

    1. God's Time      46
    2. God's on my Road Trip      47
    3. God's Assignment      48
    4. Shine God's Light      49
    5. God's Clearing my Path      51
    6. Jesus is the Captain of my Ship      52
    7. Your Prayers Alone      53
    8. Helping Hand      54
    9. I Surrender Lord 0.      55
    10. Water me Lord      56
    11. God's Portrait      58

## God's Power

    1 Mend my Heart Lord      62
    2. 3573 Promise from the Lord      63
    3. Through the Storm      65
    4. Jesus Rose      66
    5. Call on Jesus      67
    6. When we Push God Away      68
    7. Thankful Season      69
    8. Harvest God's Love      70
    9. Fallen from Grace      72
    10. There's nothing too big for God      73
    11. Higher Lord      74

## *God for us all*

1. God for us All — 78
2. Getting my Ugly on Beautiful — 81
3. Trust God — 82
4. Your Word Lord — 83
5. Illuminating Rays of Brightness — 84
6. God's Healing Power — 85
7. Grateful for — 86
8. He's Calling — 87
9. We can make it — 88
10. Blessed are the Children — 89
11. Pie in the sky — 91

## About the Author

Jacqueline James is a published author who specializes in poetry with a great passion for children's stories.

She has devoted countless hours of research along with general observation to give authentic quality to her work.

She also brings a personal touch through her own experiences in her writing to keep (you) her readers inspired.

Jacqueline is on a mission for peace and acceptance through the diversity in others.

She has chosen the KJV as a guide for structural behavior with motivations acceptable through the discipline of the gospel.

Jacqueline James has been blessed with God's voice for direction through her poetry.

FOR HIS GLORY

## The dedication

This book is dedicated to Almighty God for His Glory!
Lord, I thank You!

# Prelude

Conception of life,
In the beginning God created man and by his side God blessed him with a woman for his mate. God joined them together as one for the conception of life to replenish the earth in His image. The miraculous greatness of this process was done for His glory.

Existence through life,
Throughout the existence of one's life God's intentions were for us to worship Him through our praise. To always serve Him by aiding to others through humility and serenity.
Thus fore we would receive blessings through God grace and mercy during our struggles and difficult situations.

Eternal life,
God promised us all eternal life for believing in His word. Also for the submissive to His will.
We shall be forgiven of our sins through iniquity and for our transgressions. Our bodies shall return to dust from which we came, however our souls shall join Jesus in the heaven in which God has prepared a room for us.

JACQUELINE JAMES

Chapter One / Glorify the Lord
1 Corinthians 10:31
Romans 15:9
Psalm 50:23
Isaiah 43:7
Isaiah 48:11
Ephesians 1:6

1 Corinthians 10:31
So, whether you eat or drink, or whatever you do, do all to the glory of God.

Romans 15:9
And in order that the Gentiles might glorify God for his mercy. As it is written, "Therefore I will praise you among the Gentiles, and sing to your name."

Psalm 50:23
The one who offers thanksgiving as his sacrifice glorifies me; to one who orders his way rightly I will show the salvation of God!"

Isaiah 48:11
For my own sake, for my own sake, I do it, for how should my name be profaned? My glory I will not give to another.

Ephesians 1:6
To the praise of his glorious grace, with which he has blessed us in the Beloved.

Isaiah 43:7
Everyone who is called by my name, whom I created for my glory, whom I formed and made."

# Chapter 1
## I Glorify the Lord

1. God gets His Glory
2. I am of God…God is of me…
3. God Rock
4. Jesus is
5. Infinite Blessing
6. God is Blessing me
7. 5-Star Faith
8. God on my Mind
9. Do it for me Lord
10. God is the Author of my Faith
11. Thankful

## God Gets His Glory...

Don't stress just relax,
This too shall pass it's just a test,
You can't have a testimony without a test,
Once you pass you've been blessed,
At the end of your test you get a testimony,
Then you'll have a story for God to get the glory,
So when the trials come your way,
Embrace them all as you pray,
Know by God's grace that you were blessed to see another day.

## *I am of God…God is of me…*[1]

I am of God and God is of me-my soul is free,
I deny the shackles you try to put on me

You are the darkness beneath the scene,
Who tries to limit my eyes to see, and my dreams to dream,

God is the wanderer in my shadow,
Who walks through fire and lives forever,

You are the demise that comes my way,
Through my faith your destruction can't stay,

God is the destiny from my dreams,
I behold the beauty yet to be seen,

You are unworthy one that I knew,
I walked on water fleeing from you,

I am the creation of my master plan,
He is the universe and I am of Him

You are the darkness of my past,
None of your realm of evil did they last,

## FOR HIS GLORY

I am the brightest of my future,
God's ray of sunshine shall be my evolution.

## JACQUELINE JAMES

# God Rock...

Watch God's miracle rock,
When God starts blessing He doesn't stop,
He'll bless you from your head to your toe,
Healing your body as He go,
Every hair on your head He'll put in its place,
Leaving you blessed by His amazing grace,
From your eyes to your neck,
He'll make sure they're working their very best,
From your chest to your ribs,
Completely healing them is He will,
From your shoulders to your hands,
Totally blessings them is His plan,
From your brain through your spine,
After God heals them they'll be fine,
From your stomach to your thighs,
He'll send His healing and they're be fine,
From your legs, knees, ankle, and feet,
God is healing them as we speak,
For all your organs locked inside,
God will cure them before your eyes,
Now from your spirit to your heart,
God's love will bless them, when you do your part,
Keep your faith and don't you stop,
Because you serve a God that truly "rock"!

## Jesus Is...

When you have seen the wind, the fire, the water, and the land,
Then you have witness Jesus right hand,

Jesus is the breath in my lungs when I talk,
His every conviction is from my thoughts,

Jesus is the mother lion carrying her cubs to safety,
Jesus is deliverance to the sinners after they've been faithful,

Jesus is my relieve after I struggle for a while,
He's the happy from my smile,

Jesus is the ant walking a mile a day storing food for the winter,
Jesus is my alpha from my beginning,

Jesus is the rain drop hitting my face on a sunny day,
Jesus is my grace and mercy when I pray,

Jesus is the soldiers returning home from the war,
Jesus is the brightness of my shinny star,

Jesus is the hope for tomorrow I feel,
Jesus is the righteous way I live,

Jesus is the light through the darkness of the night,
Jesus is the reason that I continue to fight,

Jesus is the lakes and the rivers that flow,
Jesus is the storms and also the rainbow,

Jesus is my children He was willing to lend,
Jesus is my loyal and faithful friend,

Jesus is my everlasting to meet Our Father,
Jesus is my hope from the minute to the hours,

Jesus is my strength when I push on through,
Jesus is gift I share with you,

Jesus is my mother and my father,
Jesus is my prayers answered in the midnight hour,

Jesus is the song of glory that my heart sings,
Jesus is my all-and-all and everything in between.

## Infinite Blessings...

God has a well of infinite blessings,
Which are all yours just for the asking,
With God your cup will run over and over,
He shed His blood for our covenant,
Through your faith there's unlimited possibilities,
You'll reach the heavens through your accountabilities,
When we trust in God it's always good,
His words are never void or misunderstood,
We must pray with supplication and work hard,
To earn the rights of God's greatest reward,
When we accept Jesus love in every essence,
Through God's grace we'll receive His infinite blessings.

## God is Blessing me...

God is going to bless me with another spot,
When He does I'm gone to "rock",
Everything good and perfect comes from God,
All of my blessings are from what He allows,
God fills my days with harmony,
With His prefect peace He's blessings me,
He puts good people in my path,
And He intervenes on my behalf,
He opens doors for me to walk through,
And gives me an overflow with the things I do,
God is blessing me as I speak,
With the precious gift of life to say the least.

# 5-Star Faith...

I have that "filet mignon" faith,
That keeps me up praising late,
I believe in God's promise over my life,
He fights my battles so I don't have to fight,
He places good people in my path,
Who intervenes on my behalf,
Through my faith I do believe,
That everything put before me I will achieve,
He said that he would give me an expected end,
Through God's words I expect to always win,
He's rising me up to a higher level,
I'll give Him the glory now and forever.

## God on Your Mind...

You'll have peaceful times with God on your mind,
When you stay prayed up it's His grace you'll find,
There's no better feelings in this world,
When we actively seek God and purge,
God will cleanse us for our sinful thoughts,
He'll give us mercy as He bring us out,
He'll provide for us when we're in need,
If we just trust in Him and believe,
The closer He get to you without interference,
The more He'll humble your heart and spirit,
So, keep your mind stayed on Him,
His unconditional love you'll feel.

## *Do it for me Lord...*

When my life is troubled and struggles become hard,
All I ask is that You do it for me Lord,
Lead me to the rock the salvation of my life,
End my struggle Lord ease my fight,
Take me to the comfort of my Father's arms,
Where this world could no longer do me any harm,
Show me to my place of peace,
Where all of my cares and worries shall cease,
Bless me Lord with Your goodness and mercy,
Grace me God with the room that's ordained for me.

# God Is the Author of Faith...

In the beginning God took a book of blank pages of my life,
He filled it with wonders of adventures which lead me
to His light,

Each line contains my destiny,
With lots of adjectives that writes my soul free,

Through every letter spells His words and more,
Keeping me humble so that my heart is pure,

Through every sentence His 'will' was heard,
Of my life instructions through His words,

In each of the words that I have learnt,
Were filled with God's blessings that I have earned,

In each paragraph God wrote me wise,
So that I may witness His miracles before my eyes,

On every page He wrote my unique story,
Which helps me honor and give Him glory,

Through every chapter He filled me with faith,

To assure me that one day I'll enter His gate,

## Thankful...

I thank You Jesus that I may hear,
The sound of Your voice from far to near,


I thank You Jesus that I may see,
All the beauty You have in store for me,


I thank you Jesus that I may feel,
All the wonderful blessings that You give,


I thank You Jesus that I may share,
All of life treasures because You care,


I thank you Jesus for the things that You do,
You show me mercy while I'm going through,

You keep me still while You're molding me,
Delivering my soul to set me free,

I thank You Jesus for keeping my mind stayed on You,
Through Your words I know are true,

You bless me with my health and strength,
Then keep me humble so that I may repent,

I thank You Jesus for filling me with a forgiving heart,
To lend to Your people as I do my part,

You grant me peace in the midst of my storm,
While I'm cradled safely in Your arms,

I thank You Jesus for all Your love,
For preparing my soul for the Master above.

Matthew 6:9-13

Our Father who art in heaven,
Hallowed be thy name,
Thy kingdom come,
Thy will be done in earth as it is in heaven,
Give us this day our daily bread,
And forgive our debts as we forgive our debtors,
Lead us not into temptation but deliver us from evil,
For thine is the kingdom, and power, and the glory forever,
Amen

Chapter Two / Revive me Lord

1 Peter 4:11
2 Peter 1:3
Philippians 2:11
Ephesians 1:12
Jude 1:25
Romans 11:36

1 Peter 4:11

Whoever speaks, as one who speaks oracles of God; whoever serves, as one who serves by the strength that God supplies—in order that in everything God may be glorified through Jesus Christ. To him belong glory and dominion forever and ever. Amen.

2 Peter 1:3
His divine power has granted to us all things that pertain to life and godliness, through the knowledge of him who called us to his own glory and excellence,

Philippians 2:11
And every tongue confess that Jesus Christ is Lord, to the glory of God the Father.

Ephesians 1:12
So that we who were the first to hope in Christ might be to the praise of his glory.

Jude 1:25
To the only God, our Savior, through Jesus Christ our Lord, be glory, majesty, dominion, and authority, before all time and now and forever. Amen.

Romans 11:36
For from him and through him and to him are all things. To him be glory forever. Amen

## Chapter 2
### Revive me Lord

1. Empty me Lord now fill me up
2. Your Love for me Lord
3. Peace me to be Still
4. Have a Clear Heart for God
5. Empty am I
6. Restore my Faith
7. Lost Souls
8. He's a Healer
9. Please Lord Have Mercy
10. A Reason to Pray
11. My Faith is Strong

# Empty me Lord now fill me up…

Empty me Lord now fill me up,
Empty out the toxic from my heart,
Fill me with Your kindness to do my part,
Empty the wrong thoughts from my mind,
Fill me with wisdom so that I may be wise,
Empty the confusion from my head,
Fill me with Your truthful words so that I am fed,
Empty the things that will destroy my soul,
Fill me with Your 'will' to take control,
Empty me from any unkind deeds,
Fill me with righteousness please Lord please,
Empty me from my sinful ways,
Fill me with Your love this I pray,

## Your Love for me Lord…

Lord when the night falls and I lose my way,
Draw me close to You Lord as I pray,
From my desperate need Lord hear my cry,
Keep my tongue worthy from morning till nigh,
Lord give an ear to hear my Master's call,
A heart to receive Your love above them all,
Show me mercy Lord over my life,
Lighten my load as I fight,
Lord humble me gently through all You do,
Keep my heart desires stayed on You,
Lord grace me with Your presence of love,
Then prepare my spirit for my Father above

## Peace me to be Still…

I got a hole left in my heart Lord that I don't want to be filled,
I got a hole left in my heart Lord that I don't want to be filled,
I got a hole left in my heart Lord that I don't want to be filled,
Just leave me,
Just leave me,
Just leave me to be still,
Oh peace me to be still Lord,
I don't want it filled,
Peace me to be still Lord,
I don't want it filled,
Oh peace to be still Lord,
I don't want,
I don't want,
I don't want it filled,
Peace Lord,
Just peace Lord,
I don't want it filled,
Peace Lord,
Just peace Lord,
I don't want it filled,
I got a hole left in my heart Lord,
I don't want it filled,
I got a hole left in my heart Lord,

## Jacqueline James

I don't want it filled,
I got a hole left in my heart Lord,
Peace me to be still,
Just leave it,
Just leave it,
Just peace me to be still!

This hole left in my heart Lord is burning me up inside,
This hole left in my heart Lord is burning me up inside,
This hole left in my heart Lord is burning me up inside,
It's my faith,
It's my faith,
Oh Lord it's my faith,
That's keeping me alive,


I got a hole left in my heart Lord that I don't want to be filled,
I got a hole left in my heart Lord that I don't want to be filled,
I got a hole left in my heart Lord that I don't want to be filled,
Just peace me,
Just peace me,
Just peace me Lord to be still!

# Have a Clear Heart for God...

After you clear your heart,
God will fill your house,

Have a clear heart free from distractions,
Then there will be room to receive God's attention,

Remove all of your negative thinking,
Make room for the blessings that God's bringing,

Remove your insecurities and all your doubt,
Then trust God completely to bring you out,

Eliminate your lust and wondering eyes,
God will reward you for your sacrifice,

He'll deliver unto you blessings day by day,
You'll reap His unlimited mercy as you pray,

Your hope in Jesus will help you to believe,
That anything's possible with God to achieve,

JACQUELINE JAMES

Once you clear your heart God will fill your house,
Then His grace and love shall flood about.

## Empty am I...

It is I Lord...empty waiting to be filled with Your precious gift of the Holy Ghost,
Humbling myself God in order to give you the most,
Refill me Lord with humility and righteousness,
Give me an overflow Lord so I may be blessed with by Your kindness,
Fill me Lord with forgiveness through my consciousness,
Grant me peace along with great patience,

Empty am I,
From the world's temptation and corruption,
Refill me Lord with Your grace through my devotion,
Let Your light radiant through my smile,
Then the world may see that I am one of God's child.

## Restore my Faith...

Broken faith drowned with sadness upon my face,
Praying for mercy through the darkness for God's grace,
Lost of time running scare in my mind,
Scattered dreams through my hope I try to find,
Wanting to make sense of a senseless situation,
The mist of confusion lured me in without hesitation,
Now I'm trapped with an overwhelming "awe",
Can't go back, can't move forward stuck in place filled with doubt,
Searching for the right prayer to break through,
Why will God allow man to do the things that they do,
God said he gave man domain over earth,
Allowing them to take pleasure through pain while others hurt,
We're giving a conscience to decide what's right or wrong,
Our faith in God helps us to stay strong,
Through perilous times God promised never to leave or forsake us,
Restoring faith in His word I do believe I must trust.

## Lost Souls

I stepped out of my comfort zone into the deepest
of the dark holes,
In order to minister to the lost souls,
Those who've been living without hope,
Using unholy things to try to cope,
Those who've became victims of society,
Who've made worldly choices their priority,
The ones who've been lost in their own thoughts,
Without a clue on how to figure their life out,
The ones who've endlessly struggled,
Instead of Jesus they've choose multiple lovers,
The ones who've been left in the dark,
With no sense of compassion in their hearts,
The ones who are locked away going insane,
Unaware of how to call on Jesus name,
Those who are without friends, and are lonely,
Not knowing Jesus will be their one and only,
The ones who are in the streets with the blues,
Because, they haven't heard about God's good news,
The ones who are suicidal and don't want to face another day,
I teach them about God's mercy when they pray,
Those who've fallen short, and have sinned,
I teach them about God's forgiveness when they repent,
The ones who are sad, and filled with sorrow,

I remind them of Jesus "joy", for tomorrow,
The ones who are sick and despair,
I make them aware of how much Jesus cares,
Those who long to see Our Father face,
I bear witness of God's amazing grace,
These are God's people I minister to,
Lost souls that was once me, or perhaps you.

## He's a Healer...

My mother was sick, and her body was weak,
She was bed ridden and could barely speak,
She went from 100% healthy down to zero,
But, when God stepped in she wasn't sick anymore,
God healed her body from head to her toe,
This is one of His miracles the world needs to know,
I witness God's miracle as it unfold,
God healed my mother's body and blessed her soul,
He restored her health and her strength,
She was fully recovered within a week,
God restored her to happiness and prefect health,
Then she gave God the glory because she was blessed.

# Please Lord have Mercy

Please Lord have mercy on my soul,
As I humbly ask You to take control,
Please Lord have Your way,
As I humbly pray to You throughout my days,
Please Lord bless my spirit,
As I humbly ask from my heart to hear it,
Please Lord tame my tongue,
As I humbly worship Jesus Your son,
Please Lord grant me peace,
As my faith in You continue to increase,
Please Lord forgive my sin,
As I accept Your son Jesus as my best friend,
Please Lord guide my thoughts,
As my mind stay on You without a doubt,
Please Lord order my step,
As You direct my path unlike anyone else,
Please Lord show me mercy and grace,
As You prepare me to see my Father's face
Please Lord don't leave me the same,
As I humbly pray to You in Jesus name.

## A Reason to Pray

Throughout every second of the day,
There's always a reason for us to pray,

From the breath in our lungs that keeps us alive,
To the organs in our body that's functioning inside,

From the strength in our muscles that helps us to move,
To skin that cover it all beautiful and smooth,

From the thoughts in our brain that keeps us sane,
To right state of mind to call Jesus name,

From our sacred bodies that keeps us physical,
To our precious souls that keeps us spiritual,

From the people we love that we call family,
To the friends we have at each of our gatherings,

From the land we share to grow our food,
To the wild and tamed animal that we rule,

From the lakes and rivers our water flows,
But mostly for the love that our Savior shows.

## My Faith is Strong....

I refuse to allow your fear to interfere with my faith,
I put my trust in God without debate,
I serve a powerful yet merciful God,
That can work miracles before the crowd,
The God I serve can calm the ocean and the roaring sea,
He can also move mountain that are hindering me,
God will show me mercy through His amazing grace,
Through the midst of my struggle put a smile on my face,
God will lift my spirit to cry no more,
He's the great "I Am" that I honor and adore,
God will shelter me from all hurt and danger,
He will protect me from the evil done by strangers,
Because I believe in Jesus my faith is strong,
God will never forsake me or leave me alone,
He will forgive my sins so I don't remain the same,
With breath in my body I will glorify God's name,
I will lift God up with my song and praise,
He will bless my life throughout my days.

Psalm 23
The Lord is my shepherd; I shall not want.

2 He maketh me to lie down in green pastures: he leadeth me beside the still waters.

3 He restoreth my soul: he leadeth me in the paths of righteousness for his name's sake.

4 Yea, though I walk through the valley of the shadow of death, I will fear no evil: for thou art with me; thy rod and thy staff they comfort me.

5 Thou preparest a table before me in the presence of mine enemies: thou anointest my head with oil; my cup runneth over.

6 Surely goodness and mercy shall follow me all the days of my life: and I will dwell in the house of the Lord for ever.

Chapter Three / God is in Control
Romans 8:28
John 1:14
Isaiah 6:3
Psalm 21:13
Psalm 19:1
Revelation 14:7

Romans 8:28
And we know that for those who love God all things work together for good, for those who are called according to his purpose.

John 1:14
And the Word became flesh and dwelt among us, and we have seen his glory, glory as of the only Son from the Father, full of grace and truth.

Isaiah 6:3
And one called to another and said: "Holy, holy, holy is the Lord of hosts; the whole earth is full of his glory!"

Psalm 21:13
Be exalted, O Lord, in your strength! We will sing and praise your power.

Psalm 19:1
To the choirmaster. A Psalm of David. The heavens declare the glory of God, and the sky above proclaims his handiwork.

Revelation 14:7
And he said with a loud voice, "Fear God and give him glory, because the hour of his judgment has come, and worship him who made heaven and earth, the sea and the springs of water."

## Chapter 3
## God is in Control

1. God's Time
2. God's on my Road Trip
3. God's Assignment
4. Shine God's Light
5. God's Clearing my Path
6. Jesus is the Captain of my Ship
7. Your Prayers Alone
8. Helping Hand
9. I Surrender Lord
10. Water me Lord
11. God's Portrait

## God's Time...

God don't move on our time,
Hear His voice for a peace of mind,
If you want to know want God has to say,
Then peace be still and pray,
He may not come when you want Him too,
But when you need Him...He knows exactly what to do,
God knows us better than we know ourselves,
He intervenes on our behalf,
He grants us the free will to do our best,
When we put Him first above the rest,
When you acknowledge Him as your personal Savior,
He'll bless you and also show you favor,
There's no greater love you'll ever find,
That'll give you an abundance in His own time

# God is on my Road Trip....

Our God is everywhere constantly showing me that He cares,
When you're at church, God's home with me,
When I'm on a plane God's sailing the sea,
When, I'm at my doctor's office,
God's with you while you're having a cup coffee,
When you're at the beach on vacation,
God's with me at the train station,
When I go swimming God's in the pool,
And He's having a picnic with you in the mid afternoon,
God's with you lying around enjoying the sun,
While He's sharing family time with me having fun,
God's in China, He's also in Spain,
He's at home with me keeping me sane,
God's with you in streets while you're trying to be slick,
God's is in the hospitals healing the sick,
God's with you at home while you're having lunch,
God's with me during dangerous time, and this I trust:
God's with you at the movie watching the show,
God's here with me in traffic while I have a long ways to go,
God's busy crossing the sun and the moon for a full eclipse,
But He still came along with me for my road trip.

## God's assignments...

God won't give you a big assignment, if you always complaining about the little assignments,
You always want God to give you an important position,
But, first He'll give you something minuet to get your attention,
When God gave me something hot, muggy and sweaty to do,
I got a rag, and a bottle of water, and pushed on through,
Sometimes God's assignments are tedious and small,
But, you'll rise to higher heights, once you've completed them all,
So, never complain about your task at hand,
Just give God the glory after each command.

JACQUELINE JAMES

# Shine God's Light...

When your day's labor become hard,
Let the world know just who you are,
A good and faithful servant of the Lord,
Let your light shine bright and bold,
When you allow Jesus to take control,

Matthew 5:14
Ye are the light of the word. A city that is set on a hill cannot be hid.

Jesus died to cleanse our sins,
And shine His glory from within,

Matthew 5:15
Neither do men light a candle, and put it under a bushel, but on a candle stick, and giveth light unto all that are in the house.

His crucifixion pay the ultimate cost,
His light gives us prefect peace when we are lost,

Matthew 5:16
Let your light shine before men, that they may see your good works, and glorify your Father which is in heaven.

Work through faith and worship our Father on the Sabbath,
Then, He shall deliver you from all bad habits,
Let God's light shine from your heart,
Give Him the glory as you do your part,
The enemy will plot to destroy your light, your hope, and your joy,
But, there's hope through the savior Jesus Christ our Lord.

# God is Clearing my Path...

God is clearing my path,
He's eliminating the enemy on my behalf,
There are many things that tries to hinder me from my progress,
But through my faith God intervenes to show that I am blessed ,
When I can't see clearly what's right for me,
God will intercept to make my life complete,
Sometimes it's hard for me to understand,
But God controls my actions and takes command,
He changes the direction that I may be going too,
Then provides me with a new course of opportunities when He's through,
He reconstructs my thoughts to conform to His ways,
Then He leaves me with peaceful and brighter days,
So when the enemy sends me the spirit of discouraged,
God clears my path and I'm left with discernment.

# Jesus is the Captain of My Ship....

While I'm traveling through time on an extraordinary trip,
Jesus is the captain of my ship,
He knows the sail that's right for me,
He gave His life so that I could be free,
Then He rose again to watch over me,
To ensure my safe journey across His sea,
A storm may rise and flood the ship in a blink,
But peace be still I will not sink,
In depths of the oceans nor will I drown,
Cause Jesus is my personal savior that I found,
Strong the wind blow to the ship it sways,
But Jesus "will" in me, will have its way,
When the course of troubles rage the sea,
Through Jesus I'll reach my destiny,
In ocean to sea and everywhere I go,
Jesus will be with me this I know.

JACQUELINE JAMES

## Your Prayers Alone...

May God stand beside you, by your prayers alone,
Your prayers alone, your prayers alone,

May He open doors, by your prayers alone,
your prayers alone, your prayers alone,

He'll fill your heart with love, by your prayers alone,
Your prayers alone, your prayers alone,

With His peace He'll bless your home by your prayers alone,
your prayers alone, your prayers alone,

God will cure your sickness, by your prayers alone,
your prayers alone, your prayers alone,

He'll heal your body, by your prayers alone,
Your prayers alone, your prayers alone,

He fight your battles through your prayers alone,
Your prayers alone your prayers alone,

God will bless your life, through your prayers alone,
Your prayers alone, your prayers alone.

## A Helping Hand...

God Himself doesn't come down to meet our demands,
He sends His people to lend a helping hand,
He places good thoughts into His servants,
To delivery great deed to whoever shall tarry,
We will receive all of God's blessings,
Through our faith just for the asking,
When we resist the devil and refuse to settle,
God will send His people to fight our battles,
We will receive the victory from our story,
When we testify and give God the glory,
Things will work in our favor if it's in God's will.
If we keep our peace and just be still.

JACQUELINE JAMES

# I Surrender Lord...

Lord it's by my choice,
That I give You my voice,
Lord it's by Your will,
That I choose to be still,
Lord it's my troubles that will cease,
When I gain Your perfect peace,
Lord it's my mind that will change,
When I call on Your name,
Lord it's Your word,
That humbles my spirit once I've heard,
Lord it's my praise,
That keeps me blessed throughout my days,
Lord it's Your hope that I feel,
That keeps me trusting You as I live,
Lord it's Your life that You gave,
When You shed Your blood to pave my way,
Lord it's Your mercy from Your light,
That ease the struggles through my fight,
Lord it's from Your grace,
That will allow me one day to see Your face,
Lord it's in my days,
To You I shall surrender as I pray.

## Water Me Lord...

Water me Lord so that I may grow,
Into the servant for the Master to know,

Reign on me Lord with Your holy words,
For in my heart they shall be preserved,

Flood my soul with Your truths that I've learnt,
So that Your mercy over my life I've earned,

Shower me Lord with Your righteous ways,
So that I may live to glorify You in my days,

Flow through me Lord with Your precious blood,
So that I may live to honor my Father above,

Purge me Lord from my lustful thoughts,
So that Your "will" in me shall bring them out,

Wash me Lord so that I am clean,
Free from ungodliness and things unseen,

Cleanse me Lord so that I may spout,
That which is worthy of You from my mouth,

Purify me Lord with Your amazing grace,
Bless me with favor to one day see Your face!

Water me Lord so that my soul may flow,
Onto the heavens where all of God's children go.

# God's Portrait...

One day God painted a picture,
In that portrait He created your beautiful face,
From the heart of God's amazing grace,
He knew that throughout your days you would give Him glory
and honor through your praise,

In every stroke of His brush contain colors of love,
That reflects the beauty of the Master above,
Through every single line He drew your journey,
Then blessed you with mercy so you need not worry,
He painted curves swirling around great mysteries,
His words were the road map holding all life history,

In your picture He added lots of sunny days,
He filled them with hope when you trust and pray,
On your face He gave you a nice gentle smile,
With the reassurance that He would be with you the entire while,
He made your expression vibrant with youth,
Giving you wisdom to understand His truth,
He sprayed you with His image to shine and glow,
Cause you are His creation and the world will know,
The day He painted your portrait it was a masterpiece,
A priceless treasure of a humble servant who's meek.

Chapter Four / God's Power
Philippians 1:11
Ephesians 3:16
Ephesians 1:14
Ephesians 1:11
2 Corinthians 4:7
John 12:28

Philippians 1:11
Filled with the fruit of righteousness that comes through Jesus Christ, to the glory and praise of God.

Ephesians 3:16
That according to the riches of his glory he may grant you to be strengthened with power through his Spirit in your inner being,

Ephesians 1:14
Who is the guarantee of our inheritance until we acquire possession of it, to the praise of his glory.

Ephesians 1:11
In him we have obtained an inheritance, having been predestined according to the purpose of him who works all things according to the counsel of his will,

2 Corinthians 4:7
But we have this treasure in jars of clay, to show that the surpassing power belongs to God and not to us.

John 12:28
Father, glorify your name." Then a voice came from heaven: "I have glorified it, and I will glorify it again."

## Chapter 4
### God's Power

1. Mend my Heart Lord
2. 3573 Promise from the Lord
3. Through the Storm
4. Jesus Rose
5. Call on Jesus
6. When we Push God Away
7. Thankful Season
8. Harvest God's Love
9. Fallen from Grace
10. There's nothing too big for God
11. Higher Lord

FOR HIS GLORY

# Mend My Heart Lord...

We take people for granted and give them our trust,
Then eventually they'll disappoints us
They'll break our heart without any explanation,

Maybe for selfish greed on personal satisfaction,

With our heart broken and left with pain,
Only shame and failure is what remains,

We put on a persona as if we have it all together,
However the damage may cause us to get off balance,
But we don't have to tolerate others bad behavior,
Once we shift our trust to our Lord and Savior,

God will heal a broken heart,
When we surrender through prayer we've done our part,

Once the burden is lifted the heart will be mend,
Because we trusted in God's word and Jesus as our friend.

# 3573 Promises of the Lord...

There's 3573 Promises from the Lord,
To be worthy of just 'one' I'll work hard,

I'm standing on God's word,
They are the sweetest words I've ever heard,

I'm holding God to His word for the instructions in my life,
He promised me if I kept His commandments then He'll fight my fight,

He promised if I lift Him up in everything that I do,
He'll be with me every step of the way to see me through,

He promised if I let shine through me Our Father's light,
Then He'll bless my days as well as my nights,

He promised if I walked by faith, and not by sight,
Then He'll lead me to a righteous life,

He promised if I had faith as small as a mustard seed,
Then I could move mountains if I believed,

He promised if I prayed and fast, and praised His name,
Nothing in my life would remain the same,

He promised if I believe in His amazing grace,
Then one day I'll be worthy to see His face.

# Through The Storm....

How to live through the storm without an umbrella,
Keep praising God and watch times get better,

How to survive the time during perilous days,
Then honor Our Father for His life He gave,

How to keep your faith strong through trials and tribulations,
Then put your trust in Jesus and form a relation,

How to get God to heal your land,
Humble yourself then He will take command,

How to get God's blessings that's meant for you,
Then give Him the glory while you go through,

How to get pass all the sinful temptation,
Then give your life to Jesus with full dedication,

For the ones who didn't live through this storm,
Praise God for them peacefully resting in His arms.

## Jesus Rose...

God sent His only begotten son to die on the cross,
For His mercy we wouldn't go without,

In three days he rose again with all power in his hands,
To spread His love throughout the land,

He rose again on the ninth hour,
Filled with God's Holy Ghost Power,

Jesus laid down His life on that Holy day,
To give us redemption as we pray,

Only God is able to bring us through,
From all the obstacles that we go through,

Before He extended from the earth,
He walked the land healing first,

He left His peace over our lives,
To keep us humble as we fight.

## Call On Jesus...

Call on the name of Jesus late in the midnight hour,
Then pray with supplication and wait on His Holy Ghost Power,
With adoration deep love and respect,
Give God praise and honor then He'll bless us that's a fact,
He is Lord of Lord over us all,
With mercy and compassion when we call,
Everything is miraculous about God's power,
With His unconditional love for us He'll shower,
The spiritual promises will never come back void,
For whatever we need we can call on Our Lord.

## When we pushed God away...

When we pushed God away,
Satan stepped up to steal, kill, and destroy our day,
When we allow prayer to be taken out our schools,
It caused chaos which wasn't cool,
Without any spiritual guidelines or rules,
We all end up playing the fool,
When we stop disciplining our "kids",
They had no sense of value to comprehend,
This left them vulnerable for lust and sin,
Their hearts didn't desire Jesus as a friend,
They became ruthless lacking empathy,
They destroy each other without any sympathy,
Satan will control our children thoughts,
We're praying that God will drive him out,
But, first we must invite God back in,
Then, believe in our heart He'll forgive our sins,
Trust Him with our very life,
As He deliver us through our daily fight,
Praise and worship Him each day,
Humbly ask "Please Lord return to us we pray"

## Thankful Season...

This is the season to be blessed,
To give God our sorrow and the rest,
To fellowship with family and with friends,
To feel the presence of peace from within,
To come together and eat good food,
Which brings us closer, and brighten our moods,
As we allow Jesus love to come in,
We are all thankful for several things,
But, mostly grateful for the mercy God's brings,
I especially appreciate all he's done for me,
How He died in order for me be free,
How He's allowed me with the gift of life,
When I call His name He makes everything alright.

## Harvest God's Love ...

People all over the world are emotionally starved,
However Jesus has enough love for the world to harvest,

If your heart becomes empty and your days become hard,
God will show you mercy to fill the void,

Trust and believe in God's holy words,
Through your faith you will receive the blessings which you deserve,

Whenever you become emotionally detached,
Jesus love will help you to reconnect,

Through your prayers God always hear,
God will relieve your burden as He draws near,

God will extend to you His amazing grace,
Then grant you peace upon your days,


Worship God from your heart and soul,
Then allow His "will" in your life to take control,


Bless God's name through your labor,
Harvest God's love as He shows you favor.

## Fallen From Grace...

As parents we give our children our hearts,
souls and our mind,
Our love money and also our time,
Sometimes they still grow up not knowing their place,
Somewhere along the way they may have fallen from grace,
When they do it's up to us,
To lead them back to our Lord and Savior we trust,

Some of us as adults have fallen from grace,
We pray for God's mercy to find our place,
We pray to God to bring us back,
To the peace and happiness that we lack,
We try to atone the wrong that we've done,
By praying for forgiveness to God's only begotten son,

However we must do more than just repent,
The demonic spirits that hinder us we must defeat,
We must avoid any unholy temptations,
In order to form with Jesus a close relation,
We all may slip but we shall not fall,
Jesus will extend His grace upon our call,

God promised the children through each generation,
If they fall from grace Jesus will be their redemption.

# There's nothing too big for God...

There's nothing to big for God,
You're worthy of God's blessing for being His child,

God will elevate you above your shortcoming,
He will bring you to a height unlike no other,
God will rise you above your present state,
He will enhance your talents to make you great,
God will remove any obstacles that get in your way,
He will bless you with accomplishments throughout your day,
God will move a mountain in your favor,
From your devotion and your labor,
Because of your faith it's already done,
God will bring you out as more than a conqueror,
There's nothing too hard or too big for God,
Through His grace and mercy He can solve it all,
Nothing will be impossible for you to do,
When your trust is in God to see you through.

## Higher Lord...

At the start of my day 1st my washer when out,
On the very next day my furnace stopped,
Soon afterwards my house got so cold,
Until unfortunately my pipes froze,

The pressure built up and my pipes popped,
The results of all the repairs cost me a lot,

After all was said and done I didn't fret,
Because I trust that God wasn't finished yet,

So I got down on my knees,
And I asked God to have mercy please,
I prayed for God to give me another mountain to climb,
Because I guarantee with God by my side, I'll be just fine,

Please take me higher Lord in my faith,
Please Lord take me higher in my stride.

Chapter 5 / God for us all…
Psalm 96:8
Psalm 57:5
Psalm 46:10
2 Corinthians 4:6
1 Corinthians 6:20
Romans 9:23
Romans 4:20
John 14:13
Matthew 11:38
Isaiah 42:8

Psalm 96:8
Ascribe to the Lord the glory due his name; bring an offering, and come into his courts!

Psalm 57:5
Be exalted, O God, above the heavens! Let your glory be over all the earth!

Psalm 46:10
"Be still, and know that I am God. I will be exalted among the nations, I will be exalted in the earth!"

2 Corinthians 4:6
For God, who said, "Let light shine out of darkness," has shone in our hearts to give the light of the knowledge of the glory of God in the face of Jesus

1 Corinthians 6:20
For you were bought with a price. So glorify God in your body.

Romans 9:23
In order to make known the riches of his glory for vessels of mercy, which he has prepared beforehand for glory

Romans 4:20
No distrust made him waver concerning the promise of God, but he grew strong in his faith as he gave glory of God

John 14:13
Whatever you ask in my name, this I will do, that the Father may be glorified in the Son.

Matthew 11:38
Come to me, all who labor and are heavy laden, and I will give you rest.

Isaiah 42:8
I am the Lord; that is my name; my glory I give to no other, nor my praise to carved idols.

## Chapter 5
### Entertainment
1. God for us all
2. Getting my Ugly on Beautiful
3. Trust God
4. Your Word Lord
5. Illuminating Rays of Brightness
6. God's Healing Power
7. Grateful for
8. He's Calling
9. We can make it
10. Blessed are the Children
11. Pie in the sky

## *God is for us all…*

Romans 8:31
What shall we say to these things?
If God be for us, who can be against us?

Who can be against us when we have our
Lord Jesus as our savior,
Through supplication and prayer He'll show us favor,

Joshua 1:19
"Have I not commanded you?
Be strong and courageous. Do not be frightened, and do not be dismayed, for the Lord your God is with you
wherever you go."

Because, our Lord is with us, we can be brave and courageous,
Even when things are chaotic, and situations become
dangerous,

Isaiah 41:10
"Fear not for I am with you; be not dismayed, for I am your God; I will strengthen you, I will help you, I will uphold you with
my righteous right hand."

God's power is in His righteous right hand,
To extend His grace to every girl, boy, woman and man,

Deuteronomy 31:6
"Be strong and courageous. Do not fear or be dread of them, for it is the Lord your God who goes with you. He will not leave you or forsake you."

Through every struggle, and difficult times,
God will be there to give us a prefect peace of mind,

Zephaniah 3:17
"The Lord your God is in your midst, a mighty one who will save; he will rejoice over you with gladness; he will quiet you by his love he will exhaust over you with loud singing."

Sing with thanksgiving to make a joyful noise onto the Lord,
He will rejoice over you with gladness, even during the mist of your storm,

Matthew 28:20
"Teaching them to observe all that I have commanded you. And behold I am with you always, to the end of the age."

Teach to all God's commandments,
And blessings will bestow unto you through His raiment,

Hebrews 13:5
"Keep your life free from the love of money, and be content with what you have, for he has said, 'I will never leave you nor forsake you.'"

Have none other than God's pure love in your heart,
He will for fill your every need and from your life He shall never part,

Romans 8 38-39
"For I am sure that neither death nor life, nor angels nor rulers, nor things present nor things to come, nor powers, nor height nor depth, nor anything else in all creation, will be able to separate us from the love of God in Christ Jesus our Lord."

For God's love, and grace is for everyone, who believe in Him and come forth,
God's love and mercy is the same today and forever more.

# Getting My Ugly on Beautiful…

I'm getting my ugly on beautiful,
I'm talking to God clapping hands, stumping feet,
Praising shouting jumping out my seat,
I'm talking hands clapping, feet stomping,
Wig throwing getting my ugly on,
Speaking in tongues telling God I belong,
Praising dancing singing to God's song,
I'm talking running shouting crying out to the Lord,
Thanking Him worshipping Him,
With saints all on one accord,
I'm talking thanking sweating fainting,
Crying out to the Lord repenting,
To His glory my love's insane,
Getting my ugly on beautiful blessings His holy name.

## Trust God...

Man will promise you all sorts of things,
Sometimes you'll fall vulnerable enough to believe,
You can believe in man if you like,
However he'll disappoint you before the day loses its light,
Man will fill your head with a bunch of lies,
But you'll stop listening when you get tried,
When you trust in man to satisfy your desires,
Then unnecessary rhetoric may be required,
Trusting in God should be your best decision,
Because He's the only one in the blessings business,

God won't ever disappoint you or let you down,
Even through things you don't understand His love can be found,
When you put your faith in man you'll always be at odds,
However you'll stay in prefect peace when you put your trust in God.

# Your Word Lord....

Please Lord fill me with Your word,
Let my life revolve around Your word,
Lord give me an ear to her your word,
So, that it's the sweetest sound I've ever heard,
Lord give me a heart to receive your word,
So, Your love will shine through me and allow the world to see,
Lord give me a mind to know your word,
So, that my thoughts will stay on You as I trust You to see me through,
Lord give me a tongue to speak your word,
So, that Your message of truth can be heard,
Lord bless be with Your 'will' to live by your word,
Let Your 'will' in me be done by Your word,
Lord let Your 'will' be what I prefer,
Thank you Jesus for Your word.

## Illuminating Rays of Brightness....

God is shining His light through me, illuminating bright enough for the world to see,

Through my obedience God's granted
me absolute clarity,
Which blessed me with total serenity,

I thank God for His brightness on me He shines,
It brings fourth blessing with peace of mind,

He reassures me that I'm not living in veins,
By blessings me with His beauty that keeps me sane,

Thank you Jesus for choosing me,
To compose the poetry from Your beauty,

## V

# God's Healing Power....

I am a walking miracle with a testimony,
About Our Fathers amazing healing power,
When I prayed with supplication for the Holy Spirit to come down,
God healed my body from my feet, to my crown,
He blessed me with His amazing grace,
Then promised me a home in an everlasting place,
He took my sins and washed them away,
Covering me with His blood for that covenant day,
God will do for you the same as He's done for me,
He will bless you from now to eternity,
He'll heal your body and save your soul,
When you humbly allow Him to take control,
Believe in Him and call on His name,
His blessings will come and they will reign,
The world will see His miracles as they unfold,
Then bear witness to His glory that made you whole,
You must trust in God completely with that crazy faith,
He'll heal your body before it's too late,
He'll remove any sickness that's harming you,
And restore you back to health when He's through,
Now call on Jesus for your healing power,
Pray with supplication every minute of the hour.

## Grateful For...

I'll go back to work whenever I'm able,
But as of now I'm enjoying all the fruit of my labor.
Clothes on my back, shoes on my feet,
God also blessed me with food to eat,
So I'm grateful every day of the week,

Grateful for shelter with a roof over my head,
Grateful for the cushion from my comfortable bed,
Also from the warmth from my softly woven spread,
God has blessed me to be safe and warm,
While I'm in the midst of a horrific storm,

I'm thanking God for clothing me in my right mind,
Patiently waiting for my time to shine,

Grateful for the rainbows floating about,
Praising my Lord as He brings me out.

JACQUELINE JAMES

# He's Calling…

When you act in your calling,
You'll never be out of character,

Stop worrying about having a membership,
What we all need is a heavenly relationship,

God expects us to give our all-in-all,
Not to go through life doing nothing at all,

Each one of us is unique in our on special way,
We must exert our expertise every single day,

Examine yourself to see what you'll find,
That's when you'll realize you're one of a kind,

He'll connect us with each other alone life's path,
To render a good service and lend a helping hand,

God has a calling on both you and me,
Praying for "truth" will discover what it possibly could be.

# We Can Make It...

We can make it through these challenging days,
When we humble ourselves and pray,

God will be with us every step we face,
To grant us mercy through His amazing grace,

When you're in doubt or perhaps scared,
Trust in God's holy word,

It's our faith that God prefers,
When we're obedient to what we've heard,
Then we will be blessed through His holy words.

# Blessed are the Children...

Blessed are the children that have been blessed by God's hand,
Though His forgiving mercy they will understand,

Blessed are the children who glorify God's name,
For His love in their hearts shall always remain,

Blessed are the children through God's perfect plan,
He shall enrich the lives of every woman and man,

Blessed are the children to be filled with hope,
To know God's love for they shall cope,

Blessed are the children who give God glory through their praise,
God shall bless their spirits as they pray,

Blessed are the children who lift God with song,
For they bless His holy name as their days are long,


Blessed are the children filled with grace,
For they shall inherit the kingdom of God's sacred place.

JACQUELINE JAMES

## Pie in the Sky...

We're constantly searching for a piece of the "pie",
We'll be lucky to get a "crumb" before we die,

We work hard throughout life trying to satisfy our days,
However things work in harmony for those of us who pray,

Yes there's always going to be challenges along our journey,
With our trust in God there will be no need for worry,

He will deliver us through all difficult times,
Then ease our burden restoring peace of mind,

God's greatest riches will be given to those,
Who keep their faith and believed Jesus rose,

God will stay with you to provide all of your needs,
When you trust in His name pray and believe,

God will grant you riches from day to night,
He will bless your soul with eternal life,

God has the ultimate "pie" in the sky,
With infinite slices by and by.

FOR HIS GLORY

## Jacqueline James

FOR HIS GLORY

CPSIA information can be obtained
at www.ICGtesting.com
Printed in the USA
BVHW062137270122
627195BV00009B/37